I0983454

Breeding Hamsters
KW-134

Contents

Photographers: Michael Gilroy, Ray Hanson, Burkhard Kahl, Percy Parslow, Penn-Plax.

Title page: An adorable spectacled hamster, one of the many varieties available to modern hamster breeders. **Overleaf:** A black-eyed cream mother with her newborn litter.

© **1988 by T.F.H. Publications, Inc.**

Distributed in the UNITED STATES by T.F.H. Publications, Inc., One T.F.H. Plaza, Neptune City, NJ 07753; in CANADA to the Pet Trade by H & L Pet Supplies Inc., 27 Kingston Crescent, Kitchener, Ontario N2B 2T6; Rolf C. Hagen Ltd., 3225 Sartelon Street, Montreal 382 Quebec; in CANADA to the Book Trade by Macmillan of Canada (A Division of Canada Publishing Corporation), 164 Commander Boulevard, Agincourt, Ontario M1S 3C7; in ENGLAND by T.F.H. Publications Limited, Cliveden House/Priors Way/Bray, Maidenhead, Berkshire SL6 2HP, England; in AUSTRALIA AND THE SOUTH PACIFIC by T.F.H. (Australia) Pty. Ltd., Box 149, Brookvale 2100 N.S.W., Australia; in NEW ZEALAND by Ross Haines & Son, Ltd., 18 Monmouth Street, Grey Lynn, Auckland 2, New Zealand; in SINGAPORE AND MALAYSIA by MPH Distributors (S) Pte., Ltd., 601 Sims Drive, #03/07/21, Singapore 1438; In the PHILIPPINES by Bio-Research, 5 Lippay Street, San Lorenzo Village, Makati Rizal; in SOUTH AFRICA by Multipet Pty. Ltd., 30 Turners Avenue, Durban 4001. Published by T.F.H. Publications, Inc. Manufactured in the United States of America by T.F.H. Publications, Inc.

BREEDING HAMSTERS

MARSHALL OSTROW

Left: *An example of a fancy variety of hamster called a long-haired cinnamon piebald by its breeder.* Below: *Two desirable coat characters, long hair and lilac coat, are seen in this fancy hamster.*

Introduction

A good pet is the type of animal that can stand up to the rigors of being kept in captivity generation after generation without noticeably declining or deteriorating in health or appearance. The golden hamster, *Mesocricetus auratus,* is one such type of animal. In nature it must battle the elements, hunt for food and hide from or defend itself against predators; but in nature it does not have to contend with well-meaning but careless handling by children and adults, dirty cages, nutrient-poor diets and the sometimes devastating

effects of breeding brother to sister. In nature, when environmental conditions are not to its liking, the hamster can move to another location; in captivity it can't. In nature it can choose its own mate; in captivity it rarely can. In nature the mate of its choosing is not very likely to be a brother or a sister or a parent; in captivity, more often than not a hamster is paired with a very close relative.

The latter problem, inbreeding, is one of the main problems with which this book will deal. While it is inbreeding that allows a breeder to develop and fix a new hamster strain, inbreeding is also one of the most serious health problems among all animals kept as pets, especially those that are rarely if ever imported from the wild.

The owners of golden hamsters are indeed fortunate, for these small animals show unusual genetic "strength," in the face of the constant inbreeding to which they are almost always subjected in captivity. Without this special "strength," golden hamsters would never have made it as pets, for it is believed that all of the millions of hamsters seen in scientific laboratories and in schools and homes where they are kept as pets are descended from one male and three females that were captured by Dr. I. Ahroni in 1930 in northern Syria, near Aleppo. (These hamsters were taken from a location very near that from which specimens were first taken and scientifically described nearly 100 years earlier.) Descendants of the hamsters captured by Dr. Ahroni arrived in the United States in 1938. Since that first and apparently only importation, it's been a tremendous success story for this tough but pretty little rodent, in spite of the fact that there have been no documented reports of the introduction of new wild stock into the domesticated stocks of American breeders. By the careful establishment of breeding lines and the occasional outcrossing of those lines, commercial hamster breeders have managed, over the years since that first importation, to establish strong, flourishing stocks of domesticated hamsters in a variety of color and fur types.

Opposite: *A lovely young golden male hamster. The golden hamster is probably one of the most recognizable hamster varieties.*

Except for the satin fur, the fancy golden hamster at left has the same markings and color of a common golden hamster shown in the photo below.

The Golden Hamster

In nature golden hamsters are found on brushy slopes of areas bordering the Black Sea on the east and south, and eastward through Turkey, Syria and northwestern Iran. There they live in burrows as much as eight feet in length. They subsist on a variety of seeds, fruits, greens and meat such as large insects (i.e., grasshoppers) and earthworms. Much of their water is derived from their food, but they do lick dew from leaves.

An adult golden hamster is about six and a half to seven inches long including the head and body but excluding the short

The Golden Hamster

tail, which rarely exceeds about half an inch in length. Females are usually slightly larger than males, but this is not a reliable way to sex hamsters. A large female golden hamster can weigh as much as seven ounces

The hamster's color is a light golden tan on the back, head and flanks. The belly, throat and chin are generally white, and the white color typically extends laterally across the shoulders, across the posterior part of the cheeks and across the upper lip. The short forelimbs are generally white, as are the hind feet, and the white often extends from behind the shoulders laterally up the sides for a short distance. The fur is usually thick and soft, covering all parts of the body including the tops of the digits and the stubby tail.

Hamsters have enormous cheek pouches which open

A family of hamsters. Note the differences in markings between the younger and older animals.

A young dominant spot male hamster and a golden Angora male.

Some representative fancy varieties of hamsters. **Opposite, top:** *Satin cream color.* **Opposite, bottom:** *Long-haired dark gray.* **Right:** *Cinnamon dominant spot.* **Below:** *Long-haired satin cream.*

inside the lips and extend well behind the shoulders. Hamsters can store tremendous amounts of food in these huge pouches. When danger threatens, nursing females are known to stuff their pups into their pouches.

The hamster's skin is quite loose. This makes it rather easy to handle the animal by simply grabbing the skin behind the shoulders with one's thumb and forefinger. Hamsters do not seem to object to this kind of handling, and they rarely struggle when handled this way as long as they are not turned upside down.

The female hamster has between 14 and 16 nipples. Although the litter size rarely reaches 16 individuals, when this does happen the female can care for them all. Usually, though, the litter size is six to eight.

In nature golden hamsters are not gregarious animals. They usually live alone in their long burrows and frequently fight with other hamsters that intrude into their burrows or even come near the burrow opening. This is especially true of female

A flesh-eared golden hamster, often referred to as the Syrian hamster.

hamsters, with attempted copulation often resulting in the death of the male. On some occasions hamster families consisting of a female and her weaned pups can live rather close together, but fights still occur when they intrude into each other's burrows. Males generally get along better with one another than do females, but they still have fights over territory and food caches. In captivity hamsters are easily tamed, and animals of the same sex are more likely to live together in peace and harmony if they are given enough room and enough food. Even well-tamed hamsters, however, are not easy to keep together in pairs. Females have little tolerance for the presence of males except for a brief period of time during mating. There are, of course, some individual exceptions, but trouble can be avoided if males and females are not normally kept in the same cage except for breeding.

In the wild golden hamsters are mostly crepuscular (active at dawn and dusk) or at times nocturnal. During the twilight hours and during the night they forage for food, dig their burrows and mate. In captivity hamsters do have brief periods of activity during the day, but

A Chinese hamster, which is smaller than the Syrian variety.

they usually spend most of the day sleeping or resting.

In nature hamsters' activities are seasonal, being most intense during late spring, summer and early fall. They do hibernate during winter, but not for the entire season. They do have brief periods of mild activity during the cold season. In captivity where light duration and temperature are usually controlled, hamsters do not hibernate, although they do tend to be a little less sexually active during the winter months.

Left: *Coarse wood chips and shavings (but not sawdust) are good bedding and nesting materials for hamsters.* **Below:** *A long-haired hamster like this dark gray variety requires brushing and combing.*

Accommodations

While animals such as gerbils do well in captivity when kept in a habitat that simulates their natural surroundings, hamsters do not. Gerbils have been kept quite successfully in large aquaria filled with dirt. These habitats allow them to burrow as they do in nature. This works well for gerbils because they produce very little urine and their feces are quite dry and hard. Hamsters, on the other hand, do not conserve water as well as gerbils do; they emit more urine and produce moist feces. Therefore, even though hamsters are also burrowing animals, they should not be kept in a soil habitat, since the soil will have to

be changed much more often than is necessary with gerbils—and changing a soil habitat is not an easy task. In nature the hamster burrow is often longer than six feet, and the place where the hamsters retreat to defecate and urinate is sufficiently far from the nest site to avoid the disease problems that could be caused by a closer waste site.

It is important that hamsters be housed in cages that are easily cleaned. For this purpose cages made of metal or plastic are highly recommended. Cages made of wood, while they may in some cases be cheaper than good quality plastic or metal cages, are not practical for the same reasons that soil habitats are not practical. Urine-soaked wood quickly takes on a putrid odor and becomes a breeding ground for bacteria and other germs that can cause diseases not only in the hamsters but also in the household in which the hamsters are being kept. Furthermore, like all rodents, hamsters are gnawing animals, and it would not take them long to gnaw through the bottom of a wooden cage. A plastic or metal cage is easily cleaned, is light in weight (making it easy to move about) and requires very little maintenance to keep it in good condition. Metal cages are especially resistant to damage caused by gnawing, and many

different kinds of plastic cages, especially the types used in laboratories, are also resistant to gnawing damage.

The cage chosen for the hamster should be as large as possible. Hamsters tend to pile up bedding material at one site and use another location having a bare bottom as a place to urinate and defecate, thus making it easy for their keeper to clean the cage. This also means that the bedding will have to be changed less often than it would if the animals had no special place to deposit their wastes. If a hamster is kept in a 6″ × 10″ cage, as gerbils commonly are, it will be necessary to clean the cage and change the litter at least once a week and possibly more often. But given a cage measuring 10″ × 16″ or 10″ × 20″ (the size of a standard 10-gallon aquarium), the hamster will be able to single out a remote site for the deposition of its wastes, and cleaning will generally not be necessary more often than once every two weeks, providing the waste site is wiped clean several times a week.

As far as cage depth is concerned, six inches would be a minimum since hamsters spend much of their time in an upright position eating, drinking and visually inspecting or sniffing their surroundings and each other; a 10- to 12-inch depth is

A young male dominant spot hamster. Some breeders add natural furnishings to their hamster's cage. One should, however, add only safe plants; one should also take care not to crowd the cage.

Left: *Finding a hamster standing or resting on its hind feet is not unusual.* **Below:** *A hamster is curious and will not hesitate to climb a toy ladder.* **Opposite, top:** *A typical rodent, a hamster will gnaw anything, especially wood.* **Opposite, bottom:** *For safety, keep flowering plants from your pet, as some may be poisonous.*

even better. The ideal hamster cage, one that is suitable for a female and her young, is about the size of a 10-gallon aquarium.

If an aquarium is used, it should have a fitted screen top that locks in place. This will allow plenty of ventilation and still help prevent the hamsters from knocking the top off and escaping, as they are capable of doing in a shallow cage.

It will be necessary to place litter or bedding in the cage. A one- to two-inch layer of bedding is best. Don't pile it up in one corner of the cage; rather, spread it over the bottom of the cage and allow the hamsters to move it around to suit their own purposes. This presents another cage problem. Some metal cages are constructed with a wire top and sides, with only a two-inch closed barrier along the bottom edges of the sides. As

The hamster's cage must be kept clean; therefore, one must also clean any cage furnishings which have been added. A variety of furnishings, such as the wheel shown here, are available at your local pet shop.

A pigmy hamster. One of the hamster's most appealing attributes is its curiosity.

the hamsters move the material about, much of it will be scattered around the outside of the cage. Therefore, if a metal cage is used, it is best to use one having a solid back and sides, with a barrier across the front of at least three to four inches in height. Some cages are made with a removable clear plastic barrier along the cage front. This allows the hamsters to be seen more clearly at all times and does an adequate job of keeping the litter in the cage.

Some hamster keepers use coarse sawdust as litter. This is not very satisfactory, as it can easily be thrown out of the cage and tends to pack down rather tightly when wet. Urine-soaked sawdust very quickly becomes foul and, like the soil habitat or wooden cage bottom, tends to become a breeding ground for all sorts of germs.

Wood shavings make the best litter material. If economy is a factor, some old pieces of pine can be shaved down using a jack plane. The resins in pine can, however, be a problem if the hamsters chew on the bedding. In the long run it pays to buy commercially packaged bedding material. One of the most popular bedding materials is cedar shavings. These shavings are strongly aromatic and help conceal the odor of the

Above: *A hamster uses its front paws for holding food.* **Opposite, top:** *A pair of hamsters feasting on corn and dried fruit.* **Opposite, bottom:** *Very succulent foods should be given sparingly, as they can cause digestive upsets.*

hamster's droppings. However, some people find the strong odor of cedar shavings as offensive as that of the hamster droppings. Commercial wood shavings are also available in a lemon scent which few people find offensive. Neither the lemon nor the cedar odor seems to bother the hamsters. However, plain, unscented shavings will ultimately be the cheapest way

to go if you plan to breed a lot of hamsters.

Although hamsters are capable of lapping water from a dish, this is risky. The dish is easily upset. Even if it isn't upset, the hamster is likely to fill it with litter and maybe even use it as a depository for its wastes. It is best to use a conventional watering bottle. This consists of a bottle containing a cork or

Cedar shavings, and other types of bedding, are available at your local pet shop.

rubber stopper with a metal, glass or plastic drinking tube inserted into it. The bottle hangs upside down from the side of the cage by means of a special hanging clip that is generally sold with the watering bottle. If a shallow cage is used, the bottle can be mounted upside down right on the top of the cage, with the drinking tube protruding into the cage. However the bottle is mounted, it should be positioned so that the hamster will be able to lap water from the end of the tube while the animal is in a standing position. This usually means that the end of the drinking tube should be five to six inches from the bottom of the cage. A second bottle should be mounted in a lower position for newly weaned hamster pups that cannot reach the mother hamster's water bottle. It is best to use a bottle that has a metal drinking tube, usually made of stainless steel, as the hamster's gnawing habits can destroy a plastic tube and can crack a glass tube, causing injuries to the hamster's mouth.

Food can be placed either directly into the cage, on the cage bottom or in a small dish, or in a food hopper built into the cage cover or cage sides. The latter arrangement is preferred because it prevents the hamsters from piling bedding material over the food or from soaking it with urine as they sometimes tend to do when the food is placed loosely into the cage. The hopper arrangement allows the hamsters to remove one food pellet at a time. If finer food is used it may be placed in a special hopper designed for that purpose (something like that in which birdseed is placed) or it can be put into a shallow dish on the floor of the cage.

Left: *Most pelleted foods are nutritionally complete, so your hamster may not need extra diet supplements except during breeding. However, be sure to read the label on the package.* **Below:** *Nuts are very fattening and should be offered only occasionally as special treats.*

Nutrition and Feeding

For hamsters to produce large, healthy litters, it is essential that they be properly fed and nourished. While getting enough food is certainly important, getting enough of the right kinds of foods can be critical. Mistakes in providing the correct diet for a pet are easy to make. For instance, people tend to overfeed sunflower seeds to hamsters. People seem to enjoy watching hamsters sit erect and shell and eat sunflower seeds. The way the animals manipulate the seeds with their front feet fascinates the hamster-watchers, so unintentionally the

hamster winds up having sunflower seeds as a major part of the diet. There should be some sunflower seeds in the hamster's diet, but only as one minor dietary component. Sunflower seeds are very rich in fats and carbohydrates. These nutrients are essential in the diet, but too much of them (nutritionists call this a "hot diet") causes digestive disorders and obesity. The animals can become lethargic and unresponsive to outside stimuli; their longevity may be reduced; and their reproductivity may be impaired. In short, an obese hamster is generally not a very healthy hamster.

Pet food manufacturers place a lot of emphasis on proteins in the diet, and rightfully so (there are millions and perhaps billions of different kinds), for they are the main structural components of nearly all living tissue. In addition, the mammalian body contains probably several million different kinds of enzymes which are also proteins. Enzymes are catalysts that allow thousands of different chemical reactions to occur in the right cells, in the right amounts and at the right times. Just how many different enzymes there are in a hamster is not known. It is known, however, that there are thousands of them in a simple bacterial cell, and hamsters are obviously vastly more complex than the lowly bacteria.

The common factor between tissue-building proteins and enzymes is that they are all made up of genetically predetermined sequences of amino acids, and there are 20 different kinds of amino acids. The sequences have varying lengths and conformations, but all contain at least a few of the 20 different kinds of amino acids. Plants synthesize their own amino acids from raw minerals, but animals do not. In order for animals to have the correct amino acids available for protein synthesis within their cells, they must consume them in the form of proteins. An animal's normal metabolic processes, catalyzed by enzymes, break down the proteins consumed into their basic amino acids. The amino acids are stored in the cells and are available for precoded protein synthesis.

When the genetic code in a cell calls for the synthesis of a particular protein, the right amino acids must be present. Feeding hamsters a high-protein diet does not necessarily ensure that they will have the correct amino acids available for protein synthesis. A great abundance of all the amino acids except one

Facing: *A Mongolian dwarf hamster eating a piece of fruit. Variety in the diet will help keep your hamster interested in life.*

A dove satin hamster enjoying an interesting and healthy meal of fruit.

can throw the whole process of protein and enzyme synthesis out of whack; thus a seemingly well-fed hamster can suffer from malnutrition. This problem can be avoided by providing the hamster with a variety of proteinaceous foods rather than just one kind of high-protein food.

This brings us to the central matter of selecting a proper diet for hamsters. Variety seems to be the key to proper nutrition—variety not only in the kinds of protein given, but variety in all

the other nutrients: the fats, the carbohydrates, the minerals, the vitamins and the fiber. A well-balanced diet produced by a great variety of foods ensures that all of the hamster's physiological functions will be carried out correctly. It ensures that the right hormones for growth and reproduction will be produced in the right cells, in the right amounts and at the right times. A well-nourished female hamster can produce healthier offspring than can a malnourished female. The female's body provides the developing embryos with all of their nutrition. Suckling pups also receive all of their nutrition from their mother via the mother's milk. For these reasons a well-nourished mother hamster that is fed a great variety of foods will produce the very best pups.

In addition to seeing the hamsters receive a variety of each kind of nutrient, it is also important that they receive the right combination of nutrients. A diet rich in a great variety of proteins can still leave a hamster malnourished if there are not enough fats and carbohydrates in the diet. In such a case, a lot of proteins will pass right through the hamster's digestive system and come out as waste, for fats and carbohydrates have a protein-sparing effect; that is, they enable the hamster's body

When feeding more than one hamster, be sure that there is enough food to go around and that the strongest hamster doesn't intimidate the smaller ones.

to utilize consumed protein more efficiently by assisting the body in its breakdown of these raw materials into the basic amino acids needed for synthesis of the correct proteins. Fats and carbohydrates also provide the basic energy needed for the breakdown of proteins and other nutrients as well as for the functioning of all extrinsic and intrinsic activities. Without an adequate energy input, hormonal and nervous systems cannot act in concert, thus sexual behavior as well as any other kind of behavior can be seriously affected. Even proper rest can be affected by an inadequate energy input, for even sleeping consumes energy.

A diet high and varied in proteins and adequate in fats and carbohydrates can still leave a hamster malnourished if that diet is insufficient in variety and quantity of minerals. Inadequate sodium and potassium can cause neural or nervous disorders in hamsters by producing an electrolytic imbalance. This affects nearly all aspects of hamster behavior, throwing off the hormonal systems and the neuro-muscular systems.

Insufficient dietary calcium and phosphorus can have dire consequences on bone and tooth formation. Pregnancy cannot be successfully completed without adequate

calcium in the diet, and neither can lactation (milk production). Without enough dietary phosphorus much of the energy (carbohydrates) consumed by the hamster will be wasted. Iodine plays an important role in metabolism and in the functioning of the thyroid gland, which directly affects growth.

Inadequate dietary iron can have drastic effects on hamsters, causing extreme lethargy and even some anemic reactions. Iron is the most important mineral in the blood, for it allows the blood to carry oxygen to every cell in the body. Without adequate oxygen, cellular respiration is curtailed and thus metabolism, catabolism and nearly every bodily function are hampered.

Vitamins also play important roles in the hamster's diet. Many maladies in hamsters are brought on by or are mediated by various vitamin deficiencies. Vitamin A, of which the primary dietary sources are animal fat and carotene (found in yellow vegetables such as carrots), promotes good growth, helps maintain good vision and maintains the estrous cycle. A vitamin A deficiency causes estrous cycle irregularities,

Opposite: *Some prepared mixtures will provide a variety of seeds for your hamster. Pet shops offer many different brands from which to choose.*

retards growth and impairs vision (especially night vision, which is most important to nocturnal or crepuscular animals such as hamsters).

There is a whole complex of B vitamins. Some of the more familiar B vitamins are thiamine (B_1) (of which a good source is grain husks), riboflavin (B_2) (of which a good source is meat) and B_{12} (which is known as the anti-anemic vitamin). A deficiency of B_1 causes severe digestive disorders. A riboflavin deficiency can cause an upset of carbohydrate metabolism, thus affecting protein utilization efficiency and ultimately limiting growth. A deficiency of pantothenic acid upsets many different kinds of enzyme activities and can affect growth, fur color and digestion as well as many other physiological functions.

Vitamin C, also known as ascorbic acid, is one of the predominant vitamins in citrus fruits, tomatoes and green vegetables. An ascorbic acid deficiency interferes with the formation of red blood cells, can cause hemorrhages and scurvy

Occasional treats are enjoyable for your hamster as long as they are not given too often.

Apples and carrots are just a few of the many healthy supplements you can give your hamster.

and retards the healing of wounds.

Vitamin E, predominant in wheat germ and lettuce, is especially important in hamster reproduction. A vitamin E deficiency can cause irreversible sterility in males and can cause pregnant females to abort.

There are, of course, many other vitamins, of which insufficient amounts cause a plethora of debilitating maladies in hamsters and other animals.

Roughage is also an essential dietary requirement. Inadequate roughage means severe digestive disorders. Roughage provides a carrier for food material passing through the digestive system. Even though all the other nutrient requirements may be in the diet, without enough roughage the hamster will not be able to utilize very much of the food it eats. Roughage or fiber in the form of cellulose is derived from fresh vegetables in the diet.

From the information presented above it can be clearly seen that there are many interrelationships among various nutrients and vitamins and that a deficiency in any one of them can have far-reaching effects on the utilization of other nutrients.

All of this serves to emphasize the great need for variety in the diet of hamsters. Some people refer to this as the "shotgun approach" to nutrition. In a spray of shot, at least a few pellets are bound to hit the target. Similarly, most of the nutrient requirements are bound to be met if enough of a variety of foods is used in the hamsters' diet. Meeting all of their nutrient requirements inevitably means that the hamsters will grow and reproduce well and that the offspring will be as healthy as their parents. This does not sound like a very scientific approach to the problem of balanced nutrition, but it is an approach that is extensively used by commercial hamster breeding establishments, laboratories and individuals, and it obviously works quite well. A more scientific approach has not yet been developed for practical use on a commercial or semi-commercial scale. The success of this "shotgun approach," however, speaks for itself!

One of the easiest ways to get variety into the hamster diet is to use commercially packaged mixes sold as hamster food. These food mixes contain an assortment of grains such as oats, wheat, wheat germ, barley and corn. The mixes generally contain cracked corn, but some contain whole kernel corn. Also found in the commercial mixes are whole shelled peanuts, sunflower seed (both in the shell and shelled), pumpkin seeds and

numerous other small seeds. Also found in mixes are prepared foods such as rabbit pellets and egg flakes, which are made from egg yolk, corn starch and tapioca flour. These mixes seem to be as complete in their nutrient variety as any single prepared food mix can be, and for this reason they are often used as the mainstay of the hamster diet.

There are some hamster enthusiasts who never feed anything else to their hamsters but prepared food mixes. There is nothing wrong with this if one is interested only in having the hamsters survive. But there's a big difference between surviving and flourishing. On such a mix, unsupplemented by other foods and vitamins, hamsters will grow to almost full size and may or may not breed. However, if some vitamin supplements are added to the food mix and the hamsters are fed an abundance of fresh vegetables and some meat they will do better than just survive—they will flourish, reach full size, have brighter colors, display more alert behavior, and produce larger, healthier litters. Furthermore, on a steady diet of one food, even if it is a varied mix, hamsters sometimes go

Opposite: *When feeding grasses to your hamster, be sure that they have never been treated with chemicals. In addition, be sure that the type of grass given is safe for hamster consumption.*

A pair of dwarf hamsters in the wild. One is eating vegetable matter, while the other is eating a beetle grub.

through a period during which the appetite wanes. By switching to a new food such as fresh turnips and sunflower seeds or to some other vegetable with sunflower seeds, the appetite can often be restored.

There are several other kinds of prepared foods that can be given to hamsters for occasional variety. Rabbit pellets, the same kind that is part of the prepared mix, can be given to the hamster as a whole meal. Rabbit pellets are small, cylindrical food chunks

that contain a concentration of green foods and other nutrients. Rabbits, of course, relish these pellets; but hamsters also often greedily eat them. Important, too, is the fact that rabbit pellets are relatively inexpensive.

Rat pellets are a popular, nutritious and relatively cheap food used not only for rats but also for gerbils, rabbits, mice, guinea pigs—and hamsters. Rat pellets do not contain as many greens as rabbit pellets, and they are much larger. In addition to their nutrient value, they provide good gnawing exercise for hamsters and thus help the hamsters keep their continuously growing incisor teeth short and sharp.

Monkey pellets can also be fed to hamsters. They are about the same size as rat pellets, but are much moister and softer. They must be stored more carefully to prevent spoilage.

Any of the individual ingredients found in a commercial food mix can be fed alone as a dietary supplement or as a treat. For instance, grains such as barley, oats, wheat, wheat germ and whole kernel or cracked corn can be purchased individually and fed to hamsters.

Hamsters are very fond of sunflower seeds as a special treat, but these seeds should not be fed in excess. As mentioned earlier they are quite rich in fats and carbohydrates. Sunflower seeds are particularly useful for

A yellow male hamster gnawing on tree bark. Any tree bark given to hamsters should be free from poisonous chemicals.

conditioning lactating females, as they do seem to enhance milk production. Be sure, however, that once the pups are weaned extra feedings of sunflower seeds are withdrawn from the female's diet.

Another good special treat for hamsters is a supply of peanuts in the shell. It doesn't take a hamster very long to get a peanut out of its shell, and peanuts are highly nutritious. Be advised, however, that like sunflower seeds peanuts are very high in fats and carbohydrates. They should be fed to hamsters only on a limited basis.

Both peanuts and sunflower seeds serve another purpose for hamsters besides nutrition. Hamsters use the husks of both as bedding material. The shells are chewed into fine fibers and are piled in the nest.

Prepackaged mixtures of a variety of seeds are available as food for canaries and finches. These seed mixtures make excellent dietary supplements for hamsters, too. Because of their small size, these seeds are usually mixed with other foods for adult hamsters, but served alone they make a good first solid food for hamster pups.

Hamsters like to nibble on dry plant stalks such as alfalfa or hay. Alfalfa is sold at pet shops in small packages as rabbit food. In addition to eating it, hamsters may also use the alfalfa as nesting material.

Small, hard dog biscuits are useful in feeding hamsters. The biscuits give them plenty of gnawing exercise, and some of them are quite high in calcium and phosphorus, thereby promoting strong bones, teeth and claws.

Since hamsters also eat meat, some semi-soft, meaty dog foods or cat foods can also be given. The amounts, however, should be carefully controlled, because stored bits of dog or cat food can spoil rather quickly and will contaminate the entire cage.

It was mentioned earlier that hamsters are also fond of large insects and earthworms. When they are in season, grasshoppers and crickets are greedily eaten by hamsters, as are earthworms of all sizes. Crickets and earthworms can easily be cultivated or purchased for use as hamster food.

Fresh vegetables and fruits should not be forgotten, as they are an essential part of the balanced hamster diet. They are an excellent source of vitamins, minerals, roughage and certain proteins as well as carbohydrates. There are two sources of fresh vegetables for hamsters—the supermarket or produce store and local fields and meadows. Nearly any vegetable that is suitable for human consumption is also

A satin cinnamon female hamster. Note how the hamster grips the wood with the front paws.

suitable for hamsters. This, of course, is the principal advantage of store-bought produce over wild vegetation. Most people are not that good at identifying wild plants, and the chances of picking plants that can sicken or kill hamsters are not insignificant. Store-bought produce therefore is much safer and offers a very wide variety of foods. Lettuce, spinach, kale, watercress, broccoli, green beans, brussels sprouts and cabbage are good sources of the B complex vitamins and vitamin C. Carrots, turnips and beets are excellent sources of vitamin A. Citrus fruits such as oranges and tangerines are fine sources of vitamin C. Hamsters also relish bamboo shoots and water chestnuts, both of which provide a wide variety of vitamins and minerals. In addition to providing hamsters with a great variety of nutrients, vegetables also provide hamsters with a good

Clean, fresh water must be available to the hamster at all times. Pet shops sell a variety of water bottles.

A two-week-old baby hamster. Nutrition is especially important for the growth and development of young hamsters.

portion of their water requirements.

Certain weeds which grow wild in lawns, fields and meadows make good vegetable foods for hamsters. However, not only must poisonous plants such as the leaves of oak, hawthorn, most evergreens and certain kinds of wild parsley be avoided, but poisoned plants must also be avoided. Do not use as hamster food wild plants taken from areas in which herbicides, fungicides and insecticides have recently been used. The best wild plants to use as hamster food are those which can be identified easily. Dandelions, clover and chickweed are commonly available weeds that are readily eaten by hamsters. They consume the stalks, the leaves and even the flowers. Although many grasses can be used as food, they do not contain nearly the amount of nutrition found in dandelions and clover.

Cereals made for human consumption are also a good source of nutrient for hamsters.

The grains in cereals are high in B vitamins and in vitamin E. Corn flakes, wheat flakes, multi-grain flakes and bran flakes are readily eaten by hamsters. The new "natural" or granola cereals are also good for hamsters. If hamsters are being bred in the home, they can be fed many kinds of table scraps. They will eat almost any kind of vegetable or meat. Just make sure they do not receive foods that are highly seasoned or oily. Don't be reluctant to experiment with the diet. As a general rule of thumb, any unspiced food that can be eaten by humans can and will be eaten by hamsters, too.

Vitamin and mineral supplements are available for hamsters, and their use is recommended, especially if the hamsters are going to be bred. A typical hamster vitamin supplement contains thiamine (B$_1$), riboflavin (B$_2$), pyridoxine (B$_6$), B$_{12}$, panthenol, choline bitartrate, ferric ammonium citrate and niacinamide. These supplements can be given to a hamster by mixing them with the drinking water or by sprinkling them over the food. Cod liver oil or other fish liver oils also make excellent vitamin supplements. Fish liver oils are especially rich in vitamin A, and their use for breeding females is highly recommended. As mentioned earlier, vitamin A helps maintain the estrous cycle. Liver oils can be mixed directly with the food.

If your hamsters are to be fed the variety of foods that is recommended in this book rather than just the commercial diet mix alone, it is a good idea to write up a feeding schedule and adhere to it as closely as possible. This will ensure a good mix of foods and a well-balanced diet, and it tells you when to bring new foods into the diet. Feeding hamsters all of these foods seems like a lot of work, but putting the foods on a regular schedule and following the schedule makes feeding quite simple and, of course, produces the very best possible breeding results. Well-fed hamsters rarely contract diseases, for their disease resistance is kept at its peak when they receive a well-balanced diet. In the long run this makes hamster keeping and breeding an easy and rewarding pastime.

Most important to hamster health is proper food storage. Dry foods such as pellets and grains must be kept dry or they will spoil, and sometimes spoiled food cannot be detected until it has been fed to the hamsters. Then it is often too late to do anything about it. These foods should be kept in air-tight,

Opposite: *A young dominant spot satin banded male hamster.*

A chocolate roan female hamster. A bright, shiny coat is an indicator that a healthy diet is being fed.

vermin-proof containers. One of the easiest ways to draw disease-laden flies, cockroaches, rats and mice into the home is to leave pet food in unsealed containers. Cleaned out coffee cans or trash cans with tight-fitting lids make good food storage containers. Fresh vegetables and meats must be kept refrigerated until they are used—if exposed to the air, they will spoil rather quickly. If there is any reason to believe that stored hamster food has been exposed to vermin or is otherwise spoiled, it is best not to chance using it, especially with young pups which are much more susceptible to diseases than are breeding adults. Food that is suspect should be discarded, and the storage containers should be sterilized.

The method of presenting food to hamsters can be an important factor in hamster health. Simple scattering of food about the cage bottom is not recommended. Food is bound to get buried under litter or bedding material, and much of it will get mixed with feces and soaked with urine. While the hamsters usually will not eat such contaminated food, it will provide a breeding ground for disease organisms and will produce an overwhelmingly foul odor.

Placing food in a dish or shallow bowl will not, of course, guarantee that the food will not get soaked and mixed with hamster wastes, but the amount of waste deposited in the specific feeding area will be minimal, and most of the waste that does get mixed with food will be inadvertently carried there along with bits of litter as the

Hamsters will hoard food they don't eat, so be sure that your hamster is actually consuming the food you are feeding him.

Fruits and vegetables are an important part of your hamster's diet. Be sure, however, not to overfeed them to your pet.

hamsters build their nests. The feeding dish should be heavy enough to prevent the hamsters from pushing it around the cage or turning it over.

In certain kinds of cages, especially those used in laboratories or commercial breeding establishments, there are built-in food hoppers. The food is poured or placed into the hopper, which is usually built into the cage lid, and the hamsters can then pull whatever amount of food they want through a small opening at the bottom of the hopper.

A nutritious diet will help keep your hamster active and fit for breeding.

Selecting Breeding Stock

One of the main goals of hamster breeders should be to improve the quality of their stock. To accomplish this it is easier to begin with good sturdy stock rather than buying hamsters that are obviously inferior. With inferior stock, which may be only a bit cheaper to buy than good stock, five or six generations may be necessary just to bring the animals up to mediocre quality. It may take a very long time to develop a superior line.

In looking for breeding stock, only young specimens should be considered. Six-week-old hamsters are ideal. At six weeks of age they are not quite old enough to mate, and they are not too old to adapt to the new environment you will provide for them. There are two good ways to tell the approximate age of a hamster. A young adult will fit neatly across the palm of your hand, but an older specimen will be a bit larger than the palm of the hand. The insides of the ears of a young specimen are covered by a sparse layer of white fur. In an older specimen the insides of the ears tend to be hairless and shiny.

Hamsters, even young ones, should have a chunky build with a short neck and a well-rounded head. The head should not be tapered and rat-like in appearance. The ears should be set widely apart. The eyes should be prominent, dark and shiny. The fur should be short, uniformly thick and should have a bit of a gloss. The animals should be alert and responsive to outside stimuli, but they should not be jittery or nervous when you approach them.

The color of the golden hamster's back and head should be a rich, uniform golden tan. The belly fur should be uniformly white as should the fur on the feet, lower jaw and throat. A dark or nearly black elongate patch of pigment should extend obliquely from the cheek upward, terminating behind the ear. Lying ahead of this should be a white crescent that terminates just ahead of the ear, and behind the dark patch should be another white crescent that terminates in front of the shoulder. A brownish golden band should extend across the hamster's chest. There should be no long white guard hairs along the hamster's sides. Close inspection should not reveal any sort of pimples in the ears or on the snout, belly or feet. The nose should be very slightly damp, but not wet. The hamster should be eating well.

The above description is that of the ideal Syrian golden

Opposite: *A young satin dominant spot male hamster. A hamster selected for breeding must be the picture of health if it is to have healthy progeny.*

hamster. This is the basic wild type from which the fancier strains were derived. While there are several other strains available, the wild type golden hamster is the best one for the beginning hamster enthusiast. It is the sturdiest of all the strains available.

There are pink-eyed white hamsters available. These are true albinos. These hamsters lack black pigment, although there are some white strains that have black eyes and sooty-colored ears—these are not true albinos. As in most other animals carrying an albino

A light gray umbrous banded male hamster. In breeding this strain, the light gray is darkened considerably when the umbrous gene is combined.

A pink-eyed, pink-eared white female hamster and her ruby-eyed baby.

mutation, the form breeds true; that is, a mating between two albino hamsters produces only albino offspring. The albino mutation is completely recessive to the wild type. This means that if an albino hamster is mated with a normal golden hamster, all of the offspring will be golden. However, in brother-to-sister matings between those offspring, one fourth of their offspring will be albino.

One of the problems with the albino mutation is that it often carries along with it other traits that are undesirable. Many of these other traits are hidden in the form of internal physiological characteristics that cause albino hamsters to be weaker than their normally colored cousins. This weakness comes about because there are not that many albino hamsters around, and to maintain the strain they must be highly inbred. This may result in the expression of deleterious traits that otherwise are normally carried along for generation after generation without being revealed.

Since animals have paired chromosomes in all but their sex cells (sperm and ova), there are two alternate genes at each site along the chromosomes. At any given site, if one gene is dominant it will prevent an alternative recessive trait from being expressed. But when both genes at that site are recessive, the recessive trait is expressed. The chances of the latter happening in brother-sister matings are much greater than they are in matings between more distantly related animals. Since albinos are maintained by close inbreeding, other recessive gene combinations at different chromosome sites are likely to show up. These are not necessarily mutations; rather, they are merely expressions of traits that were there all along but were masked by dominant alternatives.

The same is true for any other specialized trait that must be maintained by prolonged close inbreeding. Thus the long-haired or teddy bear hamsters, panda hamsters, cream-colored hamsters and all the other specialized strains tend to be weaker than the wild type golden hamster. These are the reasons that beginners should stay with the wild type golden hamster for a while and concentrate on producing better hamsters rather than unusual hamsters.

The problems caused by brother-sister matings can be initially avoided by purchasing your males and females from two different sources. This would almost eliminate the chances of your breeders being brother and sister.

A young, black-eyed white angora hamster. Before breeding your hamster, be sure it is fully mature.

A group of young, black-eyed cream females, both normals and satins.

Breeding Hamsters

In addition to causing changes in physical appearance, domestication of animals sometimes even causes changes in behavior, such as docility or even intelligence. One of the best examples of such changes can be seen in cattle. Cattle ranchers in the midwest are forced to put up fences on some of their ranges to keep the animals from grazing on a poisonous plant called astraglia. Wild grazing animals living in the same areas seem to know instinctively that the plant is poisonous and they avoid it, but domesticated cattle do not.

Similarly, some animals seem to lose part of their instinctive defensive behavior when they are domesticated. This is often the case with the hamster. Reports on the behavior of wild hamsters indicate that the female accepts the male only during the brief period of fertility. At any other time the male is chased out of the female's burrow, and if he doesn't make a fast exit, chances are he will be killed. Domesticated golden hamsters often display the same intersexual aggressiveness, but there are many cases in which they do not. There are some cases in which males and females can live together in the same cage for their entire lives, having only occasional spats. It has even been reported that some male hamsters sleep in the nest with the female and her pups. This, however, is not usually the case. Most often the behavior of the domesticated female hamster lies somewhere between that of a wild female and that of a completely accepting domesticated female.

One of the reasons that commercial breeders keep the sexes apart is to minimize the chances of breeding males sustaining injuries during mating. Because a domesticated female hamster's peacefulness toward a male is not that reliable or consistent, it is recommended for anyone who is serious about breeding hamsters that the males and females be kept in separate cages and that breeding females be temporarily introduced into the male's cage only for the brief portion of the estrous cycle during which the female is fertile. Professional breeders indicate that there will be greater breeding success and less damage to males if the female is introduced into the male's cage rather than vice versa. This may be related to the territorial instincts of the hamster, for it is known in countless examples throughout the animal world that a territorial

Opposite: *Mature male and female hamsters should be kept separately until the female hamster will accept the male for breeding purposes. This hamster is wisely being kept alone.*

Breeding Hamsters

A black-eyed cream mother hamster with her litter of black-eyed youngsters.

animal is usually much more successful in defending itself in its own territory than it is when it wanders into the territory of another of the same kind of animal.

In order to know when to place the male and female hamster together, one must be familiar with all aspects of the female's estrous cycle. Hamsters are polyestrous animals; that is, they become sexually receptive many times during the year, whereas monoestrous animals have only one heat per year (usually in the spring). Following each heat the female hamster becomes anestrous. This is a sexually quiescent period during which the female shows no sexual interest whatsoever in the male. It is during anestrous that the chances of a female injuring or killing a male are greatest. The estrous-anestrous cycle in hamsters repeats itself about every four or occasionally five days. The female usually has her first heat at the age of eight to ten weeks and every four days thereafter throughout her reproductive life, which can last until she is about 12 months of age. Generally, the only exceptions or interruptions in the cycle are during pregnancy, during the winter when the cycle slows down somewhat due to cooler winter temperatures and toward the end of the female's reproductive life.

SEXING

In order to be able to purchase breeding hamsters and determine the timing of the estrous cycle it is necessary to know how to sex hamsters. At or near adulthood the testes of the male descend into the scrotum, causing an obvious bulge at the base of the tail. This can be most clearly seen by looking down at the hamster from above. The bulge is particularly prominent when the male is ready or nearly ready to breed. The main problem in using the scrotal bulge as a means of sexing hamsters is that the bulge is not always there. The testes can be completely retracted up into the body cavity, and they often are when the animal is under stress. It is not uncommon for the testes to be retracted when the animal is handled or otherwise frightened. By holding the hamster in the normal method

A litter of dwarf hamsters. Note the dark stripe on the backs of these babies.

(by the shoulder skin) with one hand and gently but firmly squeezing it around the middle with the other hand, the testes will usually once again descend into the scrotal sac.

While adult or young adult hamsters often can be sexed without lifting them up, a far more reliable way to sex them is to lift them up and examine their genitals. The genital area of the female has three openings. The most anterior opening is the slightly elevated urinary papilla. Just behind the urinary papilla

lies the vagina, and just behind the vagina lies the anus. In adults of most strains a darkly pigmented area surrounds the vagina and anus.

In the male's genital area only two openings will be seen, the penis and the anus. The penis lies in front of the anus and is quite prominent. On a young male, even though the testes have not yet descended, the penis is quite obvious. To be absolutely certain, however, it is best to examine a few hamsters to compare males and females.

Young littermates of opposite sexes should be separated as soon as they can be safely taken away from their mother.

A golden piebald hamster. Piebald continues to be a popular variety.

MATING

The estrous cycle in hamsters generally lasts for four days and sometimes a little longer. Every fourth morning a white discharge appears at the female's vaginal opening. Lifting the female by the loose skin over the shoulders and palming her, belly up, reveals the discharge. It may be necessary to bend the tail slightly backward to see the discharge. This white mass is the post-estrous discharge and marks the end of day two of the cycle—it follows the end of the female's period of receptivity. The receptive period begins on the evening of day one and ends on the morning of day two. By following the cycle of the female for a week or two, it will not be difficult to determine when the female should be placed with the male. The evening of day one of the cycle is the best time. This means that the female should be placed with the male on the evening of the fourth day after the estrous discharge is first detected. If the cycle seems to be running every five or six days, as it sometimes does, the female should be placed with the male on the evening of the fifth or sixth day after the discharge is

Left: *A view of a hamstery. Note the cards for recording breeding data.* **Below:** *A light gray hamster.* **Opposite, top:** *A short-haired albino female and her three long-haired albino offspring.* **Opposite, bottom:** *The piebald (center) is the first mutation to have occured in hamsters.*

first noticed. The following chart will clarify the cycle.

Healthy young hamsters from sound breeding stock should be active and curious about their surroundings.

Day	AM	PM
1	sexually quiescent	sexually receptive period begins
2	receptive period ends and discharge appears	discharge prominent, sexual quiescence begins
3	small discharge, sexually quiescent	end of discharge, sexually quiescent
4	sexually quiescent	sexually quiescent

Mating in hamsters does not occur as quickly as it does in more gregarious animals like gerbils. Females, as mentioned earlier, are likely to be quite aggressive toward males, even when they are sexually receptive This aggressiveness must be suppressed before copulation can occur. When the female is first placed in the male's cage the animals are very cautious. They begin the introduction by sniffing one another around the snout. The female may then suddenly begin to hiss or snarl at the male, and she may even attempt to bite him. As the male defends himself the female flees. However, if the female is receptive she soon returns and the sniffing begins anew. This time the sniffing occurs with more apparent interest and enthusiasm. They sniff one another on the snouts, then at the scent glands located along the ventral flanks and finally in the genital area. They may at this time sit up on their hind legs and continue sniffing each other from an erect position. The female may snarl and flee several more times, but each time the snarl is quieter and the flight slower. When the female's fleeing

Mating is preceded by sniffing, which acts as an introduction for the partners.

Above: *Banding in hamsters is seldom complete. A strip of colored hairs along the spine persists.* **Opposite, top:** *A satin cream banded pregnant female.* **Opposite, bottom:** *In the hamster, the band is often incomplete and irregular, as seen in this golden umbrous specimen.*

behavior slows down the male follows her, sniffing her in the genital area as they move along. At this point the male usually begins to vocalize by emitting a soft panting sound. This sound indicates his readiness for direct sexual contact and serves to stop the female's flight behavior. The female now presents her hindquarters to the male, and he wastes no time mounting the female; thus a copulatory series begins. As is typical of so many members of the family Cricetidae, multiple intromissions are necessary before ejaculation can occur. Typically, hamsters have about 10 intromissions prior to the beginning of multiple ejaculations. The female may then behave peacefully toward the male for a while, but often by morning her aggression toward him again begins to increase. She should be removed from the male's cage as soon as possible after the completion of the sex act.

CARE DURING PREGNANCY

The pregnant female should be disturbed as little as possible, for stress during this 15- to 16-day period could have dire consequences in the development of the young. Stress during pregnancy could cause development birth defects or could even cause the female to abort.

Cleaning the female's cage and changing the litter while she is in the mating cage with the male will eliminate at least one major disturbance. The cage will have to be cleaned one more time (other than the usual wiping up of the waste area every few days) before the babies are born. That major cleaning should occur on the eleventh or twelfth day of pregnancy. This will then give the female plenty of time to build a new nest before the pups are born. At this time the female should be handled more gently than she is normally. She should not be picked up in the usual manner. In fact, she should not be handled at all. To remove her from the cage, lure her into an empty coffee can or some sort of a small box that has been baited with food. Once she crawls in, the trap should be gently turned upright and removed from the cage. After the cage is cleaned and new bedding and fresh water are provided, place the trap back into the cage and gently turn it on its side so that the female can crawl out—do not dump her out! When the female begins to build her nest, additional litter or bedding material can be added to the cage at the nest site.

During pregnancy and during the nursing period a richer than normal diet should be provided. More high-protein foods such as nuts and carrots should be used

The back stripe, a characteristic of the dwarf or Chinese hamster (a distinct species quite different from the Syrian hamster), is already evident on this youngster.

and more sunflower seeds (but not too many) or some other source of fat should be offered. In addition, some milk will be appreciated, as it will help ease any pain the female may experience during nursing. (The calcium in milk promotes better lactation.) Milk can be offered either in the drinking bottle, mixed with the food or in a separate small, shallow bowl. Be sure to remove unconsumed milk or milk-soaked food before it spoils. It should not remain in the cage for more than a couple of hours.

CARING FOR THE PUPS

The litter usually consists of an average of about eight pups.

They are about an inch long at birth and are completely hairless. They are quite pink in color, and their eyes are closed.

The pups can wiggle about very slowly and feebly at birth. During the birth process they may become scattered around the nest. However, once all the pups are born, the mother will gather them into the nest. She does this by using her teeth to pick them up by the loose shoulder skin. Even if a pup seems to be dead, do not put your hands into the cage at this time. If a pup is dead, the mother will either eat it or remove it from the nesting area (and you can remove it later, after she has settled down with her brood). If

Above: *A long-haired satin cinnamon hamster. The satin fur is very lustrous but it tends not to be as thick as the normal fur.* **Opposite, top:** *The eyes of these twelve-day-old hamsters should be opening soon.* **Opposite, bottom:** *A good sow stays close to her young and, by constant grooming, keeps their coats in immaculate condition.*

the female is frightened during most of the nursing period, she may react by eating her pups. Therefore, no attempts should be made by the hamster breeder to handle the pups.

At about seven days of age the pups will be covered with a sparse coat of dark hair. These are the guard hairs. A few days later the golden fur will begin to appear.

When the young begin to crawl from the nest at about 12 days of age, they are seeking food other than their mother's milk. At this time they can be given some soft foods such as carrot or celery tops or rolled oats. Be sure there is some water available for them. The watering bottle should be lowered enough for the pups to reach it, or some water can be placed into a small dish. Make sure the dish is shallow enough to permit the pups to crawl out of the water should they fall in during their feeble attempts to drink. Also, for the same reason, the water in the dish should not be more than an eighth of an inch deep; otherwise the pups could drown if they fall in.

At about 15 days of age the pups' eyes will open and the fur will be well developed. The cage can now be given a thorough cleaning. The mother and the pups should not be separated during the cleaning, or there could be trouble when they are put back together. The mother will continue to nurse her pups until they are about 21 days old, and that is the best time to separate her from her brood.

The pups can be reared together, but the sexes should be separated by the time the hamsters are four to five weeks old. This will help prevent fights and will eliminate the possibilty of brother-sister matings. Just after weaning, pups from other broods can be combined in a larger cage for rearing, but the sexes should be kept apart. After about four weeks of age, new youngsters should not be brought together, for to do so will cause many fights to break out. When cleaning the rearing cage, all of the pups should be removed together. Their absence from one another for more than a short while (sometimes just a few minutes) will, upon their reintroduction, cause them to act as strangers to one another, and some serious fights and injuries could result.

Young hamsters (whether they are pushed in a carriage or not!) should be separated, by sex, when they are four to five weeks old.

Left: *A dominant spot mother and her litter of dominant spot and self-colored pups.* **Below:** *A successful mating occurs only if the female is ready to breed.*

Selective Breeding

Improvement of one's hamster stock is accomplished by a process of selection favoring desirable qualities and eliminating inferior or deleterious qualities. Selective improvement is not as difficult as it sounds, and it does not require expertise in the field of genetics. It merely takes a lot of patience, a keen eye and some very elementary knowledge of the laws of inheritance.

Producing better hamsters can be accomplished in two ways. One is to select for desirable

Before a hamster is bred, it should be in good physical shape and should have had plenty of exercise.

traits such as a rounder head, a chunkier body or a more distinct color pattern. This would be done by mating hamsters that both carry the desired traits or at least are known to be able to pass those desired traits on even though the animals themselves don't show the traits. The other method is to select against undesirable traits by preventing two animals that both show the undesirable trait from breeding together or by preventing hamsters known to be able to pass those traits on from breeding with one another.

While inbreeding has been discouraged in order to minimize the number of inherited defects in hamsters, selective breeding to fix or improve a desirable trait or to eliminate an undesirable trait invariably requires a good bit of inbreeding. It seems that inbreeding is a necessary evil. Breeding close relatives together, as explained earlier, increases the chances of having inferior or deleterious characteristics show up in the offspring. But inbreeding works the same way for desirable traits, and this is why selective breeding requires a good eye on the part of the hamster breeder.

One of the best ways to fix a desirable trait is to breed brothers and sisters, each carrying that trait, to one another. This offers the greatest opportunity for improving a trait, although at the same time offers the greatest opportunity for producing other undesirable traits. The chances of producing undesirable traits can be reduced a bit by breeding offspring back to their parents and grandparents rather than to each other. Unfortunately, this practice also decreases the probability of improving or fixing the desired trait. However, in a parent-offspring mating or a grand parent-offspring mating the probability of the offspring having both the desirable and the undesirable traits at the same time is less than it would be in a brother-sister mating. Thus the desirable trait can be

A lovely cream Angora hamster. Breeders continue to improve the various hamster coat types.

Above: *Selective breeding plays an important role in the development of a beautiful fancy variety hamster like this lilac dominant spot.* **Opposite, top:** *An albino (pink-eyed) sow and her litter of cinnamons.* **Opposite, bottom:** *A new strain of white (black-eyed) hamster.*

Selective Breeding

fixed in a sibling-parent or sibling-grandparent mating, but it will take a little longer than it would in a sibling-sibling mating scheme.

A typical breeding scheme to fix a desirable trait would work something like this: Starting with a totally unrelated pair, two breeding lines are established. This is done by breeding the best female offspring back to her father and the best male offspring back to his mother. The initial stock would be known as the parental (P) generation. The first generation offspring would be known as the first filial (F_1) generation. Breeding the F_1 offspring back to the P generation establishes two lines of F_2 offspring, line A and line B. From the F_2 offspring of line A select the best male and breed it back to its grandmother. From the F_2 offspring of line B select the best female and breed it back to its grandfather. This produces F_3 offspring in line A and line B.

For the next stage of the mating scheme the parental generation is eliminated. The F_1 offspring become the grandparents to which the F_3 offspring are mated. Since it was the female F_1 that was used to establish line A, it is this line A animal that should become the grandmother. Conversely, it was the male F_1 that was used to establish line B, and this animal should be used as the grandfather. From the F_3 offspring of line A, select the best F_3 female in line B and breed it back to the F_1 grandfather. To keep the lines organized, just remember that once a grandparent has been bred its usefulness to the scheme is finished, and it should be disposed of or given away.

In theory this scheme could continue forever, but in reality it cannot, for hidden undesirable traits are bound to show up once in a while. The best way to eliminate these problems once they occur is to establish a new P generation by cross-mating the breeding lines or by introducing some altogether new stock (outcrossing). While the latter alternative may produce the best strengthening of the breeding line, it is the least desirable alternative, since it will not carry the trait that has been improved over the first few inbred generations. Linecrossing, however, usually does the trick in eliminating the new undesirable trait if the breeder has been keenly observant and caught the problem the very first time it appeared.

In a situation such as this, prevention is a lot easier than cure. Genetic deterioration can often be prevented by taking the initiative to outcross or linecross on a regular basis and at approximately every fourth

A satin golden tortoiseshell hamster, one of the many interesting hamster varieties.

Above: *A hamster with a rough coat is called a rex. This variety also has bent or wavy whiskers.* **Opposite, top:** *A chocolate banded roan hamster. The band on this hamster is very wide.* **Opposite, bottom:** *This tortoiseshell satin hamster would be rejected by a serious breeder because of its poor markings.*

generation. This will usually head off inbreeding trouble before it begins.

In selecting offspring for the breeding scheme, the differences between them can sometimes be very subtle. Once a desirable difference is spotted, that animal should be marked, because that difference could change as the animal matures. Furthermore, other members of the litter might develop that same trait a week or two later. Dye markers or even felt-tip pens having ink that is not water-soluble can be used to mark the selected hamster. The mark should be made in a place that is

conspicuous enough to be seen without disturbing the hamster too much but inconspicuous enough that it doesn't spoil the animal's appearance. One of the best spots is inside the ear. The problem with dye marking, however, is that it is usually not permanent.

A more permanent method of marking a hamster for identification is to cut a tiny notch in the thin outer edge of the ear. Notches can be cut at different locations along the edge of the ear, or multiple notches can be used to identify different hamsters in the same brood. A special notching tool is

A golden hamster. Before breeding a hamster, be sure it is physically mature.

A pair of flesh-eared albino hamsters. One should have some experience before attempting to breed albinos.

available, although a simple fingernail clipper can be used. If the notch is cut no deeper than about $\frac{1}{16}$ of an inch, there will be no nerve or blood vessel damage and the procedure will not cause any pain for the hamster. The cutting tool should be sterilized before it is used (either by dipping it in alcohol or by briefly heating it).

After a couple of generations and the establishment of number of breeding and maintenance cages, hamster breeding can become rather complicated. Mistakes can be made quite easily when dealing with a great

Above: *A tortoiseshell hamster. This character is linked with the animal's sex. It is not, however, a lethal trait.* **Opposite, above:** *Two black hamsters and a roan hamster.* **Opposite, below:** *Closeup of a black baby hamster. Note the lack of light-colored hairs among the pure black ones.*

number of animals. In a breeding program like this, one mismatch can throw all of your progress out the window in one fell swoop, wiping out a year or two of intensive work. Therefore, it is essential to keep records. In addition to marking the animals, their cages should bear clearly written identification tags which provide information such as the line symbol, the generation symbol, the date of birth, the number of times the animal has been bred and an identification of the trait or traits it is being bred for. Furthermore, a diary or a record book should be kept, noting all the information on the cage tags and filling in all the details including any defects noticed or ailments the animals are treated for. In addition, an outline of the future breeding scheme should be kept in the record book.

Breeding hamsters can be a fun, rewarding experience. The thrill of watching the babies grow into adulthood must be experienced to be believed.

Index

Breeding Hamsters
KW-134